A DAY IN AN ECOSYSTEM

24 HOURS IN A SALT MARSH

CHRISTY PETERSON

Cavendish Square

New York

Published in 2018 by Cavendish Square Publishing, LLC
243 5th Avenue, Suite 136, New York, NY 10016

Copyright © 2018 by Cavendish Square Publishing, LLC

First Edition

Website: cavendishsq.com

This publication represents the opinions and views of the author based on his or her
personal experience, knowledge, and research. The information in this book serves as
a general guide only. The author and publisher have used their best efforts in preparing
this book and disclaim liability rising directly or indirectly from the use and application
of this book.

CPSIA Compliance Information: Batch #CS17CSQ

All websites were available and accurate when this book was sent to press.

Library of Congress Cataloging-in-Publication Data

Names: Peterson, Christy, author.
Title: 24 hours in a salt marsh / Christy Peterson.
Other titles: Twenty-four hours in a salt marsh
Description: New York : Cavendish Square Publishing, [2018] | Series: A day
in an ecosystem | Includes bibliographical references and index.
Identifiers: LCCN 2016048265 (print) | LCCN 2016051381 (ebook) | ISBN
9781502624796 (library bound) | ISBN 9781502624765 (E-book)
Subjects: LCSH: Salt marsh ecology--Juvenile literature. | Salt
marshes--Juvenile literature.
Classification: LCC QH541.5.S24 P48 2017 (print) | LCC QH541.5.S24 (ebook) |
DDC 577.69--dc23
LC record available at HYPERLINK "https://lccn.loc.gov/2016048265" https://lccn.loc.gov/2016048265

Editorial Director: David McNamara
Editor: Fletcher Doyle
Copy Editor: Rebecca Rohan
Associate Art Director: Amy Greenan
Designer: Stephanie Flecha
Production Coordinator: Karol Szymczuk
Photo Research: J8 Media

Printed in the United States of America

CONTENTS

DAWN

THE morning sun peeks over the mountains and lights the tops of tall evergreen trees behind you. You watch as light spills over the land and across the bay. A bright blue kingfisher hovers over shallow water near the shore. It dives, headfirst, and pops back up with a small fish in its bill. Three cormorants roost nearby. They hold their wings out to dry in the rising sun.

The ground beneath your feet is slippery mud. You smell salt in the air and hear gulls calling. But no waves roar in from the ocean. Instead, the water laps gently against the shore. You are standing in a salt marsh on Nehalem Bay, Oregon, on the Pacific Ocean.

Salt marshes are a kind of **wetland**. A wetland is land that is soaked or flooded with water. Most wetlands are under water for weeks or even months at a time. Salt marshes are different. They flood and empty with salt water as ocean **tides** rise and fall. Some parts of a salt marsh

The sun rises over the salt marshes on Nehalem Bay.

Nehalem Bay lies on the Oregon Coast.

are under water twice a day at high tide and dry again at low tide. Other areas only fill with water during the highest tides—perhaps a few times a month or sometimes just once or twice a year.

Salt marshes take root near quiet, protected water. There are no crashing waves to wash away soil and plants. Often salt marshes form where wide, lazy rivers meet the ocean. Others are found where islands offshore protect the coast from the pounding surf. The salt marshes on Nehalem Bay are protected from the waves by a strip of land that stretches out between the bay and the Pacific Ocean.

Salt marshes can be found around the world. Some are as tiny as a backyard. Others stretch for miles and miles along the shore. Some have warm, pleasant summers and rainy, cool winters. Others shift from sweltering summers to icy winters and back again.

No matter the size or the weather, salt marshes are home to many **species** of plants and animals. In fact, salt marshes can support as much life as rich farmland. In some salt marshes, you might see a tall, pink, roseate spoonbill wading at the water's edge. In others, you might see a floating alligator or a shy bear. Salt marshes are home to fish and turtles, hawks and crabs—even sharks.

The salt marsh you are about to explore is a thin strip of land between Nehalem Bay and a dense, evergreen forest. The bay is surrounded on three sides by land, which protects it from the ocean waves. Mud flats stretch out between the marsh and the water. Grasses and other plants fill the marsh. Pale gray driftwood, pushed ashore by the water, is scattered over the ground. The noisy honk of a great blue heron fills the air.

Mud and grass, logs and herons, all the living and nonliving things you see around you make up the salt marsh ecosystem. What life will you discover here? Grab your mud boots and watch your step. It's time to find out.

In tropical areas, mangrove swamps grow along quiet shorelines.

WHERE IN THE WORLD?

Two regions in the world do not have salt marshes. In tropical areas near the equator, mangrove swamps grow in quiet, protected coastal areas. Unlike salt marsh plants, mangrove trees cannot survive freezing temperatures. You also will not find salt marshes in Antarctica. The weather there is too harsh for salt marsh species.

MORNING

THE salt marshes on Nehalem Bay average around 75 inches (191 centimeters) of rain per year. During today's adventure, though, you can pack away your raincoat. Pull on a hat and sunglasses. It is September, and the cool autumn rains have not begun.

It is always a good idea to bring a friend when you explore. The most important thing in a salt marsh is to keep an eye on the tide. See it creeping up higher and higher? It fills the bay like a giant bathtub.

Life in a salt marsh depends on these tides. Twice a day, every day, water seeps over the marsh's muddy banks and up long, narrow **channels**. Suddenly, it stops. Slowly, the water creeps back again. It sinks lower and lower until there are wide, muddy flats between the water and the marsh plants.

Why does water in Earth's oceans rise up and fall back twice a day, every day? There are two main causes. They are gravity and centrifugal

At high tide, much of a salt marsh is under water.

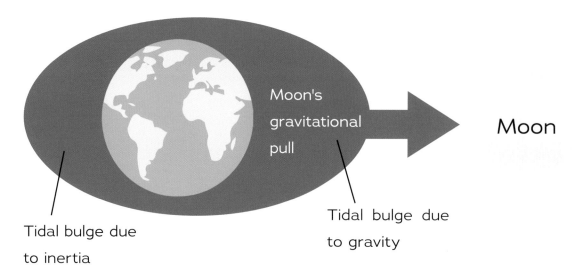

Moon's gravitational pull

Moon

Tidal bulge due to inertia

Tidal bulge due to gravity

The tides are affected by a combination of gravity, centrifugal force, and inertia. As Earth spins, the affected areas change.

force. Gravity causes things to move toward each other. Centrifugal force causes things to go outward from the center of a spinning object.

The pull of gravity on the oceans comes mostly from the moon. (The sun has a much smaller effect, because gravity's pull goes down as things get farther apart, and the sun is much farther from Earth than the moon.) On the side of Earth closest to the moon, the moon's gravity pulls on the oceans. This causes water in the oceans to bulge out, which creates a high tide.

However, Earth and the moon also revolve together around a center of rotation. To picture what "center of rotation" means, imagine a person

(Earth) holding a rope with a ball attached (the moon) and spinning in a circle. The point where the mass of the person and the mass of the ball balance is called the "center of rotation." Because of centrifugal force, the water in the ocean wants to move away from this center. This makes a second bulge, or high tide, on the opposite side of the Earth from the moon. Inertia keeps the water bulging, overcoming the moon's gravity, which is lower on this side of Earth because the moon is farther away.

As Earth rotates, the area closest to the moon changes. The result is that the two bulges move.

There are 24 hours in an Earth day—scientists call this a solar day. But tides do not follow the solar day; they follow the lunar day. A lunar day is the time it takes for a place on Earth under the moon to rotate around to that same spot under the moon. A lunar day lasts 24 hours and 50 minutes.

There are two high tides and two low tides in a lunar day; they happen about 12 hours and 25 minutes apart. This means that high tide and low tide happen at different times each solar day. Today's first low tide happened just before sunrise. Now the water moves slowly back toward the marsh, but there is enough time to explore the mud flat.

Crouch down low. See the long, green strands sticking out of holes in the mud? Pick up one of the strands. It looks like grass, but it is a kind of algae.

Many everyday products, like this cosmetic face mask used for reviving skin, contain algae.

ALGAE EVERYWHERE

You probably eat algae every day! They help make ice cream creamy and thicken jams, mayonnaise, and sauces. Algae are also used in products like shaving cream, lotion, toothpaste, and makeup. If you see "agar" or "carrageenan" on a label, that product contains algae!

Algae are like plants in many ways. They make their own food from sunlight and a gas called carbon dioxide. But unlike other plants, algae do not have roots, stems, leaves, or flowers. There are many kinds of algae in the mud flats and the salt marsh. Tiny **diatoms** live in the mud and water. Each diatom is a single cell with a tough outer covering. You can only see them with a microscope.

Other algae are easier to see. The brown slime on a nearby rock is algae. The thin green sheet that looks like lettuce—also algae. The clump of seaweed washed up on the shore? You guessed it! Seaweed is an algae, too.

The water has started to lap around your boots. Time to get to higher ground. The edge of the marsh is a thick bank of soil and partially rotted plants. Before you step up, take a small handful. Do you notice a strong smell? The color and smell come from tiny **bacteria**. These bacteria are able to live in the marsh soil, even though it does not have much oxygen. They

In Nehalem Bay, three-square sedge grows in the lowest part of the salt marsh.

breathe another kind of gas called sulfur instead. The bacteria give off a gas that smells like rotten eggs. Pee-yew!

The bacteria might be smelly, but they have an important job. They break down dead marsh plants. This allows nutrients from the plants to go back into the soil. These nutrients provide food for new plant growth.

Plants are constantly dying back in the marsh, making way for new growth each spring. The bacteria do not work fast enough to break down all this material. The plant layers pile up, forming a thick, rich soil called peat. This is why the marsh is higher than the mud flats.

You hop up onto the bank. Beside you, the tide fills a low channel. The channel winds through the marsh, all the way back toward the forest. Channels form in a salt marsh where freshwater from creeks and salt water from the bay carve paths through the peat. Channels are the lowest part of the marsh and are the first area to fill when the tide comes in.

Tall, green stems grow out of soft mud in the channel. You reach out to feel one of the stems. It is thick and strong and has three sides. The plant

Pickleweed turns bright red in autumn. It grows with salt grass

WILD GROCERIES

Mice and birds eat pickleweed seeds, but pickleweed is also eaten by people. In early spring, you might find fresh pickleweed stems at a grocery store. Pickleweed is sometimes called sea asparagus or sea beans. It can be eaten fresh in salads, steamed, or pickled.

is three-square sedge. Its hollow stems store oxygen for its roots. It gets rid of extra salt through its long, slender leaves. Look closely, and you can see salt crystals sparkling in the sun. These adaptations allow it to survive being under water for much of the day. It can grow in the lowest part of the marsh, where no other plants can grow.

A low plant that looks a bit like a cactus grows around your feet. The tips of its fat stems glow red in the morning sun. Growing alongside this plant is a short grass with fan-shaped stems. These two plants are pickleweed and salt grass. Salt grass gets rid of extra salt through its leaves, just like sedges. Pickleweed stems hold extra water. The extra water dilutes the salt so it will not hurt the plant. When too much salt builds up, the stems turn red and break off.

Three-square sedge, pickleweed, and salt grass grow in the low marsh. The low marsh floods every day during high tide. As you move to higher ground to escape the rising water, you

The seeds of marsh grasses are food for birds and small mammals.

see different grasses and flowers. Large clumps of tufted hairgrass have turned golden. The aster still has a few purple blossoms. You can see yarrow plants, with their lacy leaves and dried up flowers.

These plants grow in the **high marsh**, which only fills with water during **spring tides**. Spring tides occur when the sun, moon, and Earth line up in a row. This happens twice a month, around the time of the new moon and the full moon.

On the edge of the marsh, where the forest and the grasses meet, you find a row of huge, silvery-gray logs. These logs are dead trees that have been pushed to the highest part of the marsh during fierce winter storms. The water will not reach this high today. It is the perfect place to stop for lunch.

AFTERNOON

THE noon sun shines bright overhead. The low marsh is completely flooded. Water fills narrow channels that wind through the high marsh. Pools of water scattered across the marsh are again connected to the bay—at least until the tide goes out again.

You are not the only one eating lunch. Nearby, a bright green grasshopper clings to a blade of grass. Grasshoppers have mouthparts that allow them to chew the leaves and stems of plants. This grasshopper is a female. Her abdomen is thick—it's full of eggs. Soon she will lay her eggs in the ground.

Next spring, tiny grasshoppers will hatch from the eggs and begin to feed on fresh, new grass. A grasshopper nymph is a perfect meal for bird chicks. A baby bird is food for a raccoon. We call the connection between the grass, the grasshopper, the baby bird, and the raccoon a **food chain**.

Most animals in a **community** eat more than one kind of food. This means they are part of more than one food chain. Many food chains

 Channels bring water from the bay further up into the salt marsh.

Grasshoppers eat marsh grasses and are food for other animals.

joined together are called a **food web**. A food web connects all living things in the salt marsh community.

A food web starts with plants. Plants use water, energy from the sun, and a gas called carbon dioxide to make their own food. This process is called **photosynthesis**. Because they make their own food, plants are called "producers."

Animals are next in a food web. They cannot make their own food—they have to eat plants or other animals. Because of this, they are called "consumers."

At the end of a food web are the **detritivores** and the **decomposers**. Detritivores are animals that eat **detritus**—tiny bits of rotting plants and dead animals. Decomposers are bacteria and **fungi**. They break down dead plants and animals and release nutrients that plants can use to grow.

Time to stow away your lunch bag and explore more of the high marsh. You might be done eating, but all around you, animals are looking for their next meal. Nearby, a long-jawed orb weaver spider has built its web across a channel.

Fungi get their food from dead plants.

Jumping spiders escape high tide by climbing up marsh plants. They spin bags to escape weather and predators.

JUMPING SPIDER

Animals have to adapt to salt marsh floods, just like plants. A jumping spider escapes the rising water by climbing to the top of a plant. Jumping spiders do not make webs to catch their food. They do spin tiny shelters, like sleeping bags, to hide from **predators** and bad weather.

Below the spider web, a fly walks on top of the shallow water. How can a fly walk on water? Simple—**surface tension**. Surface tension happens when water meets air. Water wants to stick to other water, but not to air. This creates a layer that acts like a skin on top of the water. Small, light animals like flies can walk on the water because they are not heavy enough to break through this layer.

The fly had better watch out though. The wolf spider wandering along the edge of the channel is light enough to walk on water too. Wolf spiders do not build webs like orb weavers. They wander through the marsh looking for insects to eat. The fly sees the spider and takes off into the air,

Wolf spiders can walk on water because of surface tension. This allows them to stalk prey such as light insects.

right into the orb weaver's web. Caught! The orb weaver rushes over and wraps the fly in layers of strong silk. The wolf spider will have to look for another meal.

Along the edge of the marsh, a song sparrow perches on a large chunk of driftwood. Song sparrows are small, striped birds. They live in the marsh all year round. Song sparrows build their nests near the ground in shrubs and grasses. They feed their chicks insects, spiders, and other marsh creepy-crawlies. In the fall, winter, and spring, they eat the seeds of marsh grasses and sedges.

Grasshoppers and song sparrows eat green plants and seeds, but most other salt marsh animals here depend on a different food source. What is it? Look out over the marsh on this early autumn day. Grass is turning brown and starting to fall over. Winter wind and rains will pound the grass into a thick, flat layer. By next spring, that layer will be broken down into smaller bits called detritus. This detritus is food for many animals in the salt marsh.

Scoop up a handful of soil from beside one of the shallow pools. The muck in your hand is home to millions of living things too tiny to see. If you had a microscope, you could see bacteria and fungi releasing chemicals to break down plant cells into smaller pieces. The tiny living things feed by absorbing these smaller pieces into their bodies.

Fiddler crabs are common in salt marshes along the Atlantic Ocean.

FIDDLER CRABS

Salt marshes in the Eastern United States are home to fiddler crabs. These crabs feed by scooping mud into their mouths. They swallow detritus, bacteria, and algae, and spit out the mud. Male fiddler crabs have a large claw, which they wave to attract females.

There are other creatures in your sample. The tiny clear creature about the size of a comma is a copepod. Copepods are shrimp-like **crustaceans**. They burrow through the mud, eating bits of detritus and diatoms. You might also see wriggling worms. Some are smooth and some have bristles down their sides.

A great blue heron uses its long, spear-like bill to catch fish and other small animals.

Your shadow falls on the pool, and a creature darts to the other side. Can you see it? It is a tiny fish—a three-spined stickleback about as long as a pink eraser. The copepods and worms in your hand are its food. The stickleback is the same color as the bottom of the pool. This camouflage helps it hide from predators.

The great blue heron at the edge of the marsh eats small fish like the stickleback. Its long legs allow it to wade in shallow water. It stares down patiently, its neck curved close to its body. Suddenly, it stabs the water with its dagger-like bill and pulls a small fish out of the water. It spins the fish into its mouth with a toss of its head and swallows it headfirst.

The energy provided by salt marsh detritus feeds the heron and the fish, the copepods and the bacteria. Not all the detritus stays in the marsh though. Let's move back out onto the tidal flats to see where the detritus goes next.

EVENING

EARLY in the evening, the sun sinks lower in the sky. The tide has almost reached its lowest point. Trees cast long shadows over the marsh. Behind you, a deer creeps out from the forest and begins to graze on tufted hairgrass.

You walk out on the mud flats. As you walk, tiny animals hop out of your way. Many people call these creatures sand fleas, but they are not insects. They are crustaceans called amphipods. Try to catch one—they are speedy!

An amphipod looks a bit like its relative, the shrimp. It has a curved, thin body and a hard outer covering called an **exoskeleton**. Amphipods are found all over the world. Some species prefer the water; others like to live on land. The amphipod in your hand is a land-dweller. It hides in burrows or under clumps of seaweed during the day to protect itself from drying out. At night, the amphipod will emerge from its hiding spot to feed. What does it eat? Detritus!

Gulls and brown pelicans rest on tidal flats just beyond the salt marsh..

Amphipods are food for many animals in the salt marsh.

Amphipods are not the only mud-flat dwellers the salt marsh feeds. Worms, copepods, and other **invertebrates** eat detritus, too. These animals are about to be food for some out-of-town visitors.

A flock of Baird's sandpipers lands nearby and skitters along the mud flat. They probe the mud with their beaks, hunting for amphipods and worms. These shorebirds have just arrived on the Oregon coast from their nesting grounds in the Arctic. The salt marsh is a safe place for them to eat and rest before they continue their 9,000-mile (14,500 kilometer) journey to their winter home in South America.

Salt marshes along the coasts of North America are important **habitats** for **migrating** birds. Many bird species nest on wide, treeless plains in the Arctic. In autumn, they journey thousands of miles to their winter homes. Some species arrive on the Oregon

AMPHIPOD MOTHERS

Female amphipods have pouches, like kangaroos and opossums. The pouch protects the amphipod's eggs until they hatch. A pouch can hold just a few eggs or a few hundred. Newly hatched amphipods stay in their mother's pouch for a few days before leaving to find food. Young amphipods look just like adults, only smaller.

Baird's sandpipers visit the salt marsh during spring and fall migration.

coast and stay all winter. Other species stay a few days or weeks. They stop again on their way north in the spring. Though these birds are part of the community for only a short time, the salt marsh is important for their survival.

The sun dips low on the horizon, turning the sky pink and orange. You hear the hum of fishing boats as they pull up to a nearby dock.

In September, anglers on the Oregon coast fish for salmon. Salmon in Nehalem Bay are resting before continuing their journey into their home rivers and streams. While they rest, their bodies change so they can return to freshwater.

Next spring, young salmon will journey from rivers and streams that flow into Nehalem Bay on their way to the ocean. They will stop in Nehalem

Chinook salmon rest in Nehalem Bay before heading upriver to spawn. The salmon smolt stop in the salt marsh to feed while on their way to the ocean.

Leopard sharks can survive in the channels of a salt marsh.

SHARKS IN THE SALT MARSH

The salt marshes in Elkhorn Slough in California host very special guests in spring and summer: sharks. Leopard sharks come into the slough to give birth. Young sharks cruise the channels in the marshes, feeding on fat innkeeper worms that hide in the mud.

Bay while their bodies change—this time so they can live in salt water. When the tide is high, young salmon hide in the salt marsh to escape predators. They gobble up detritivores and other tiny marsh creatures. The abundant food helps the young salmon grow bigger, stronger, and more likely to survive the open ocean.

Salt marshes provide food and resting spots for migrating birds and fish. They shelter and feed young fish until they are big and strong enough to move to deeper waters. All these animals spend time in a salt marsh. But some ocean food chains that begin in the salt marsh end with creatures that never set foot or fin in the marsh.

Walk right to the water's edge. Do you see the water moving? **Currents** take the marsh detritus from the quiet waters of the bay out into the Pacific. The rotten bits of plant become food for some kinds of **zooplankton**. Zooplankton are tiny animals that float on the surface of the ocean. Though they can move, they are not strong enough to push against the currents.

Zooplankton are not just one kind of animal. Some zooplankton can only be seen with a microscope. Others, like copepods and amphipods, can be observed with a magnifying glass. Some zooplankton stay small

Tiny zooplankton are food for many ocean animals, although they may have come from the salt marsh.

their entire lives. Others are newly hatched fish, jellyfish, and other sea life. These animals will eventually grow big enough to swim on their own.

Some zooplankton eat detritus. Others, like krill, eat diatoms, algae, and other zooplankton. Zooplankton are food for many ocean animals, from

The largest animal on earth, the blue whale, eats zooplankton.

small fish to the largest animal ever to live on earth—the blue whale. Adult blue whales grow to about 85 feet (26 meters) long. Their hearts are the size of small cars. They migrate along the coast, from California to Alaska and back again. Along the way, they eat 4 tons (3.6 metric tons) of krill per day.

From the United States to South America, from a sheltered bay to the open ocean, from grass to amphipods to birds, from rotting plants to tiny zooplankton to the largest animal on earth, the salt marsh food web reaches across land and ocean.

In the low light of the setting sun, you turn to step up the bank. It will soon be too dark to see well. The big log in the high marsh is the perfect place to watch and listen. While everyone else sleeps, you watch and wait.

NIGHT

NIGHT falls. You pull out a flashlight and shine it into a pool in the high marsh. A dark shape scuttles under a chunk of driftwood in the pool. You lift the wood and gently pick up the small crab hiding underneath.

The crab peers at you from under your curled fingers. Its round eyes sit at the top of two short stalks. You shine your flashlight on the crab to get a better look. Its pale-green exoskeleton is speckled with light and dark spots. There are short hairs on its ten legs.

You are holding a yellow shore crab. These crabs hide in burrows and under logs during the day. They come out at night to feed on diatoms and algae. Feeding at night is safer for crabs because the shore birds that like to eat them are asleep.

Not all the predators are asleep. You hear a rustle in the grass and find a hiding spot behind the log. A dark shape trundles out of the grass. In the low light, you can see it wade into the pool. It searches the bottom of the pool with its paws.

The yellow shore crab hides in burrows and under logs during the day but comes out to feed at night.

Curiosity gets the best of you, and you switch on your flashlight. Bright eyes shine in the beam. The animal is the size of a small dog and has a black mask. A raccoon! Startled by the light, the raccoon slinks back into the grass.

Raccoons are **omnivores**. This means they eat plants and other animals. In the autumn salt marsh, a raccoon can find seeds of grasses and sedges. In the spring, there are bird eggs. Shrubs on the edge of the

Raccoons find many kinds of food in a salt marsh.

marsh have berries. Crabs and other sea life can be found year-round.

You scramble back up on the log. The tide is sneaking back up the shore. Along with the tide, a young English sole moves into the marsh to feed. Its flat body hugs the bottom of the marsh as it hunts copepods and other tiny mud creatures. As they get bigger and stronger, English sole move out into the bay and finally out into the Pacific Ocean.

Some English sole are caught by another member of the salt marsh food web—humans! In fact, many of the fish and shellfish people eat, like salmon, sole, cod, and smelt, spend part of their lives in the salt marsh.

The wind picks up. You pull out a sweatshirt. The sky is still clear, but it will not be long before winter brings high water and strong winds to the bay. Storm water will reach the high marsh and toss the huge driftwood logs like sticks.

Young English sole live in a salt marsh before moving to deeper water..

STRANGE EYES

An English sole is a kind of flatfish. A flatfish starts life with eyes on each side of its head. After hatching, one eye starts moving toward the other. Both eyes end up on one side of the fish, and the fish spends the rest of its life lying on the opposite side.

Salt marshes protect shorelines from violent storms.

Thousands of miles away, a hurricane slams into the Florida coast. Sidewalks crumble and boats are tossed up on the shore. However, in places where salt marshes line the coast, damage is reduced. Salt marsh soils soak up water like a sponge. The wide swaths of grass and other plants absorb the energy of the storm. By the time the surging water reaches past the high marsh, it cannot do as much damage.

Salt marshes also clean water coming into the ocean. Often rain rushing down streets and into streams becomes polluted with oil, chemicals, and other harmful materials. As the water winds through the marsh, the spongy soil of the marsh filters out these pollutants.

From your perch on top of the log, you see the sky begin to lighten. The quiet night sounds give way to the cheery calls of salt marsh birds.

Behind you, a song sparrow bursts into song. You hear a robin chirping. Then a chickadee joins in—chick-a-dee-dee-dee.

Another day in the salt marsh is about to begin. The tides will roll in and out. Animals will find food and shelter. The salt marsh will continue to help people, too. It will provide food and shelter for fish we eat. It will protect us from storms. It will filter pollution out of water.

We have only recently begun to understand how important salt marshes are to us. In the

Great egrets hunt fish and other small animals in the salt marsh.

The song sparrow lends its voice to the dawn chorus.

THE DAWN CHORUS

Around sunrise, many birds sing more loudly and longer than at any other time of day. Scientists are not sure why birds do this. It may be that male birds use this time to try to sing better than other males around them.

past, people thought salt marshes were wasted land. They cut down salt marsh grasses for hay and used them as pastures. They built barriers along the marshes to prevent them from flooding. They filled them in with dirt and built buildings on top.

The salt marsh in Jamaica Bay ouside of New York City is recovering, thanks to the efforts of many people.

Now that we realize how important salt marshes are, people around the world are working to save them. Groups of people from huge government organizations to small neighborhoods are buying up salt marshes to protect them from development. They are removing barriers to allow water back into low coastal areas. They are bringing in soil and replanting grasses and other salt marsh species.

In the late 1990s, the Jamaica Bay salt marsh in New York City was rapidly disappearing. City, state, and national government groups came together to help. Neighbors, students, birders, and surfers volunteered to plant thousands of marsh plants. Boat captains ferried the volunteers back and forth.

Thanks to all this hard work, visitors flying into New York City can look down on the marsh as their planes land. They might spot a tall, white great egret wading in the shallow water or a flock of shore birds flying low over the mud flats. With a little help, salt marshes around the world can recover and spread. Animals and people alike will continue to benefit from this amazing ecosystem.

WHERE ARE OUR SALT MARSHES?

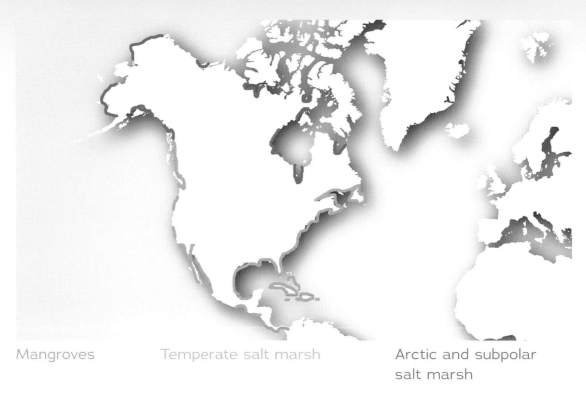

Mangroves   Temperate salt marsh   Arctic and subpolar salt marsh

FAST FACTS ABOUT SALT MARSHES

Location: Salt marshes are found in temperate regions around the world and in the Arctic. They are not found near the equator or in Antarctica.

Size: Salt marshes come in all sizes, from the size of a backyard to thousands of acres. There are several salt marshes on Nehalem Bay. Together they total around 600 acres (243 hectares).

Temperature: Temperatures in a salt marsh vary depending on location, season, and whether it is night or day. Salt marshes can be found in places where it gets below freezing in the winter. They are not found in tropical areas where it stays hot year-round. On Nehalem Bay, temperatures rarely get above 80 degrees Fahrenheit (27 degrees Celsius) or below freezing (0°C).

Rainfall: Precipitation in a salt marsh depends on location. Nehalem Bay is located in the Pacific Coastal Temperate Rainforest, a region that stretches from Northern California to Alaska. Average rainfall on Nehalem Bay is about 75 inches (190 cm) per year.

Plants Found in Pacific Salt Marshes: *Low marsh*: three-square sedge, saltgrass, pickleweed, arrow-grass, seaside plantain, spike-rush, and jaumea. *High marsh*: saltgrass, pickleweed, jaumea, slough sedge, Baltic rush, tufted hairgrass, meadow barley, Pacific silverweed, marsh clover, aster, yarrow. There are also many kinds of algae, bacteria, and fungi.

Animals Found in Pacific Coast Salt Marshes: *Insects and spiders* include grasshoppers, katydids, butterflies, dragonflies, mosquitoes, midges, flies, long-jawed orb weavers, jumping spiders, and wolf spiders. *Crustaceans* include yellow shore crabs, Dungeness crabs, amphipods, copepods, and isopods. *Mollusks* include sea slugs and clams. *Fish* include three-spine stickleback, salmon, sole, anchovies, smelt, flounder, lingcod, rockfish, perch, and sculpin. *Birds* include Western gulls, Western and Baird's sandpipers, killdeer, common mergansers, mallards, American goldfinches, violet-green and tree swallows, great egrets, great blue herons, belted kingfishers, savannah sparrows, song sparrows, American robins, northern harriers, marsh wrens, red-tailed hawks, Virginia rails, sora, American crows, and cormorants. *Mammals* include raccoons, black-tailed deer, elk, mink, muskrats, grey foxes, river otters, weasels, deer mice, vagrant shrews, Townsend's voles, bobcats, and coyote. There are also *mites* and *worms*.

GLOSSARY

adaptation A change in a living thing that helps it survive conditions in the surrounding environment.

algae Plantlike organisms that are usually found in or near water.

bacteria Simple life forms made of one cell.

channel An area cut out of the land by moving water.

community The plants and animals living together in an ecosystem that depend upon each other for survival.

crustacean An animal that has a hard outer shell, or exoskeleton, several pairs of legs, and usually lives in or near water.

current The constant movement of ocean water caused by tides, wind, and the rotation of Earth.

decomposers Organisms that break down dead plants and animals so nutrients are available for other plants and animals to use.

detritivores Small animals that feed on dead, rotting plants and animals.

detritus Dead and decaying plants and animals.

diatom A kind of algae that is made of up one cell and has a tough, outer covering.

ecosystem All living and non-living things that exist and interact in a particular area.

exoskeleton The hard, protective outer covering of invertebrates.

food chain A food chain shows how food energy moves from one organism to the next.

food web Overlapping food chains—a way to show that most organisms eat more than one kind of food and belong to more than one food chain.

fungi A group of organisms that have features similar to plants and animals. Fungi are decomposers. Some fungi eat living plants and animals.

habitat A place where an animal finds shelter, food, water, and a place to raise its young.

high marsh The area in a salt marsh that is under water only a few times a year. Plants in this area have a lower tolerance for flooding and salt.

invertebrates Animals that do not have an internal skeleton.

low marsh The area in the salt marsh that is flooded at high tide. Plants in this area have adapted to survive flooding and high levels of salt.

migrating Moving from one area to another. Many animals migrate. Some migrate short distances; others move thousands of miles.

nutrients Substances that animals and plants need to live and grow.

omnivores Animals that eat plants and other animals.

photosynthesis The process plants and algae use to make food using sunlight, carbon dioxide, and water.

predators Animals that get their food by killing and eating other animals.

sedge A plant, similar to grass, that grows near water or in wet ground.

species A type of plant or animal.

spring tides Tides that occur during a new moon and a full moon. During a spring tide, there is the biggest difference between high and low tide.

sulfur A yellow element found commonly in nature as a solid or a gas.

surface tension A property of the surface of water and other liquids that causes it to behave as if it is covered with a thin film or skin.

tides The rising and falling of the oceans each day due to the interactions between Earth, the moon, and the sun.

wetland Areas where soils are saturated all or part of the year.

zooplankton Tiny animals or the young of larger animals found in freshwater or salt water. Zooplankton are weak swimmers and usually drift along with the currents.

FIND OUT MORE

Books

Alber, Merryl. *And the Tide Comes In ... Exploring a Georgia Salt Marsh.* Lanham, MD: Taylor Trade Publishing, 2012.

Johansson, Philip. *Marshes and Swamps: A Wetland Web of Life.* Wonder Water Biomes. Berkeley Heights, NJ: Enslow Elementary, 2007.

Kurtz, Kevin. *A Day in the Salt Marsh.* Mount Pleasant, SC: Sylvan Dell Publishing, 2007.

Wechsler, Doug. *Marvels in the Muck: Life in the Salt Marshes.* Honesdale, PA: Boyds Mills Press, 2008.

Websites

What is a Salt Marsh?

https://www.youtube.com/watch?v=3HXyTMnj7ac

Biologist Susan Adamowicz, from the Rachel Carson National Wildlife Refuge, shares information about salt marshes.

What is a Wetland?

http://www.nwf.org/Kids/Ranger-Rick/Animals/Mixture-of-Species/What-Is-A-Wetland.aspx

This is a short primer on wetlands from *Ranger Rick.*

What Makes a Wetland a Wetland?

http://www.nwf.org/~/media/PDFs/Eco-schools/WhatMakesaWetlandaWetland-2.ashx

This resource from the National Wildlife Federation talks about all kinds of wetlands, including salt marshes.

INDEX

Page numbers in **boldface** are illustrations.
Entries in **boldface** are glossary terms.

ABOUT THE AUTHOR

Christy Peterson has written books, articles, and words for museum exhibits for kids and families. Her favorite things to write about are animals that other people think are strange or scary. Christy and her family live in Washington State, just two hours from the Pacific Ocean. When she is not writing, she enjoys hiking, camping on the Oregon coast, knitting hats, and cuddling with her pug.

PHOTO CREDITS